This book belongs to:

I Can Draw & Color Christmas Fun!

Mary Lou Brown & Sandy Mahony

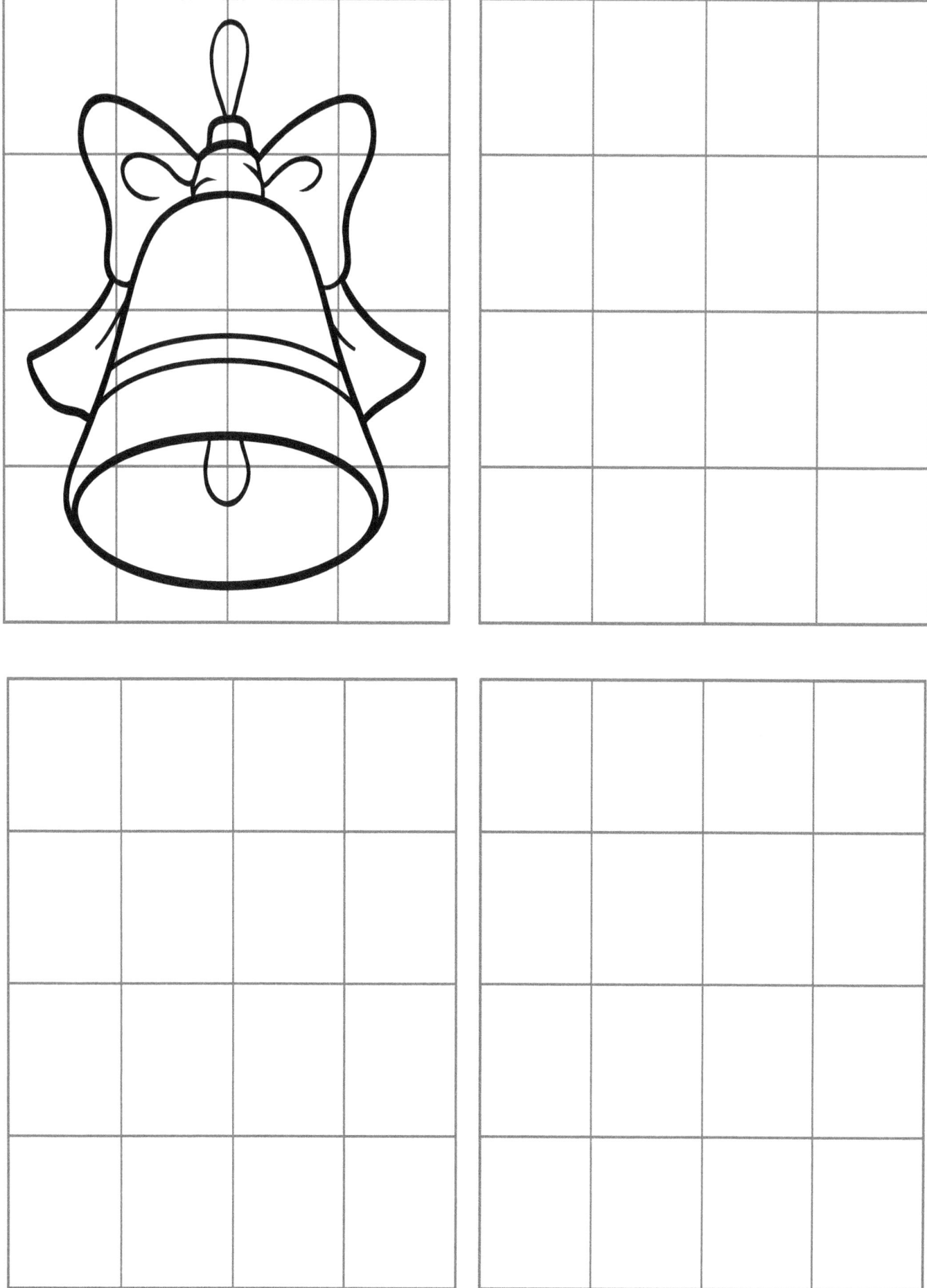

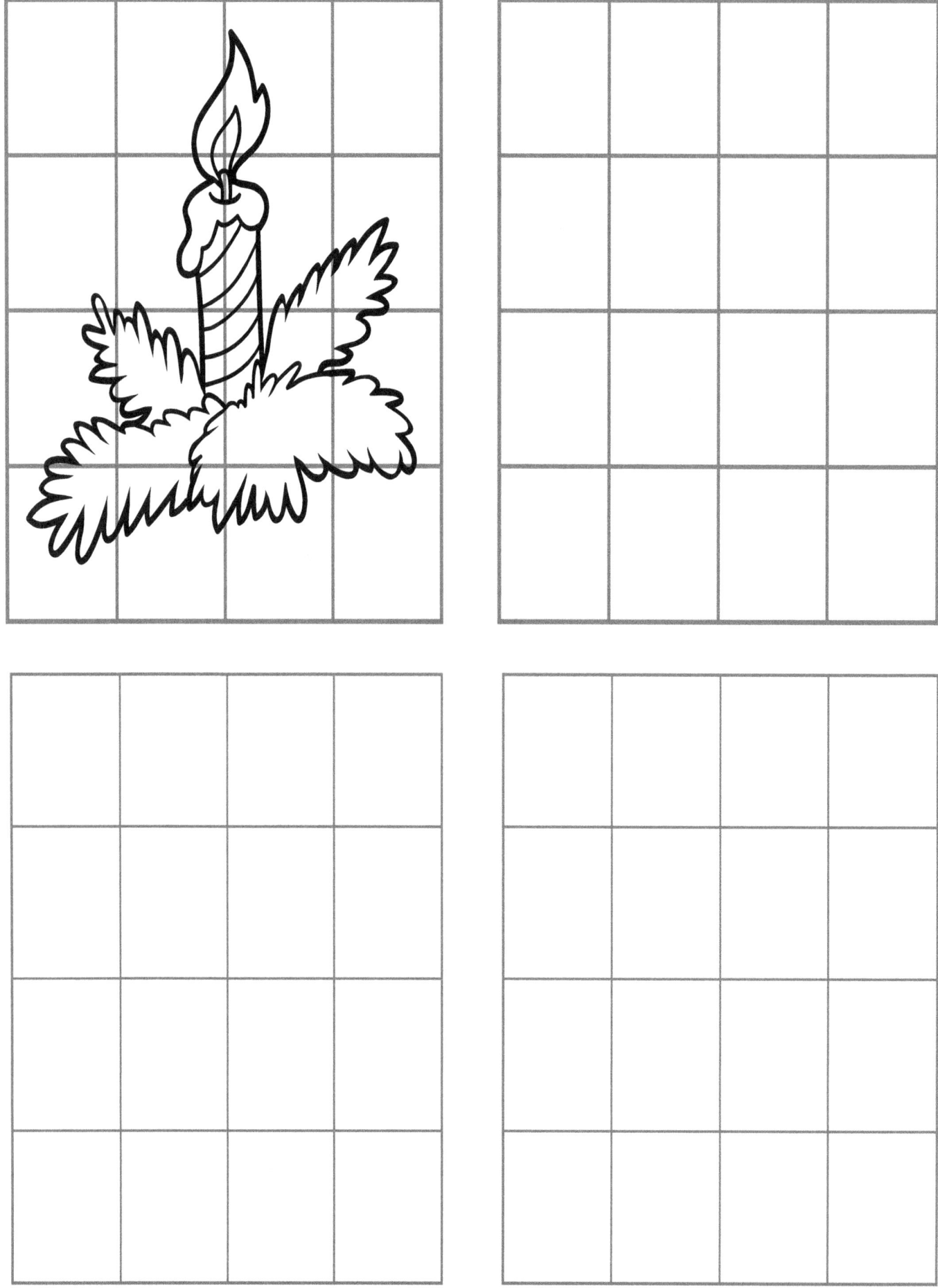

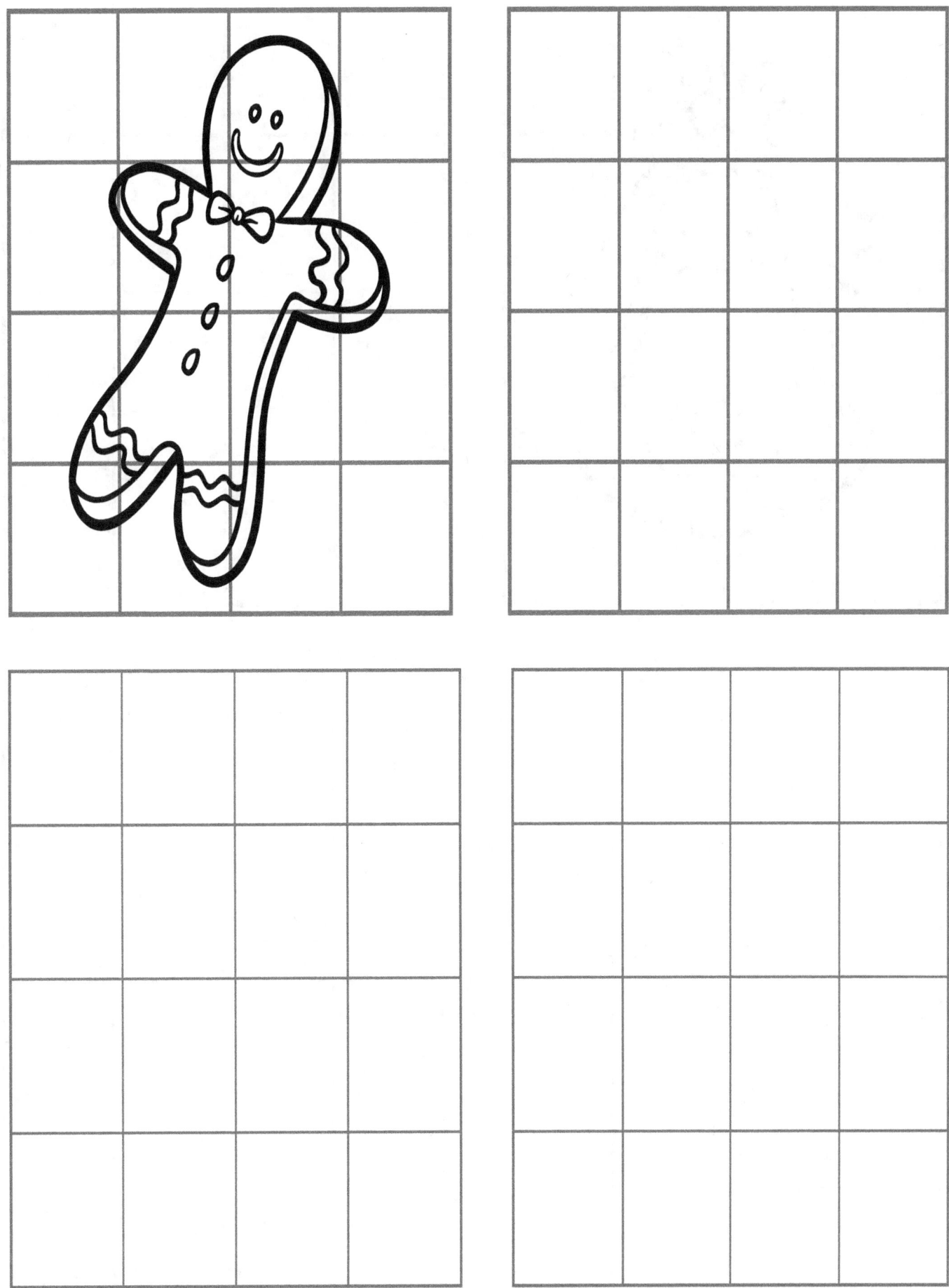

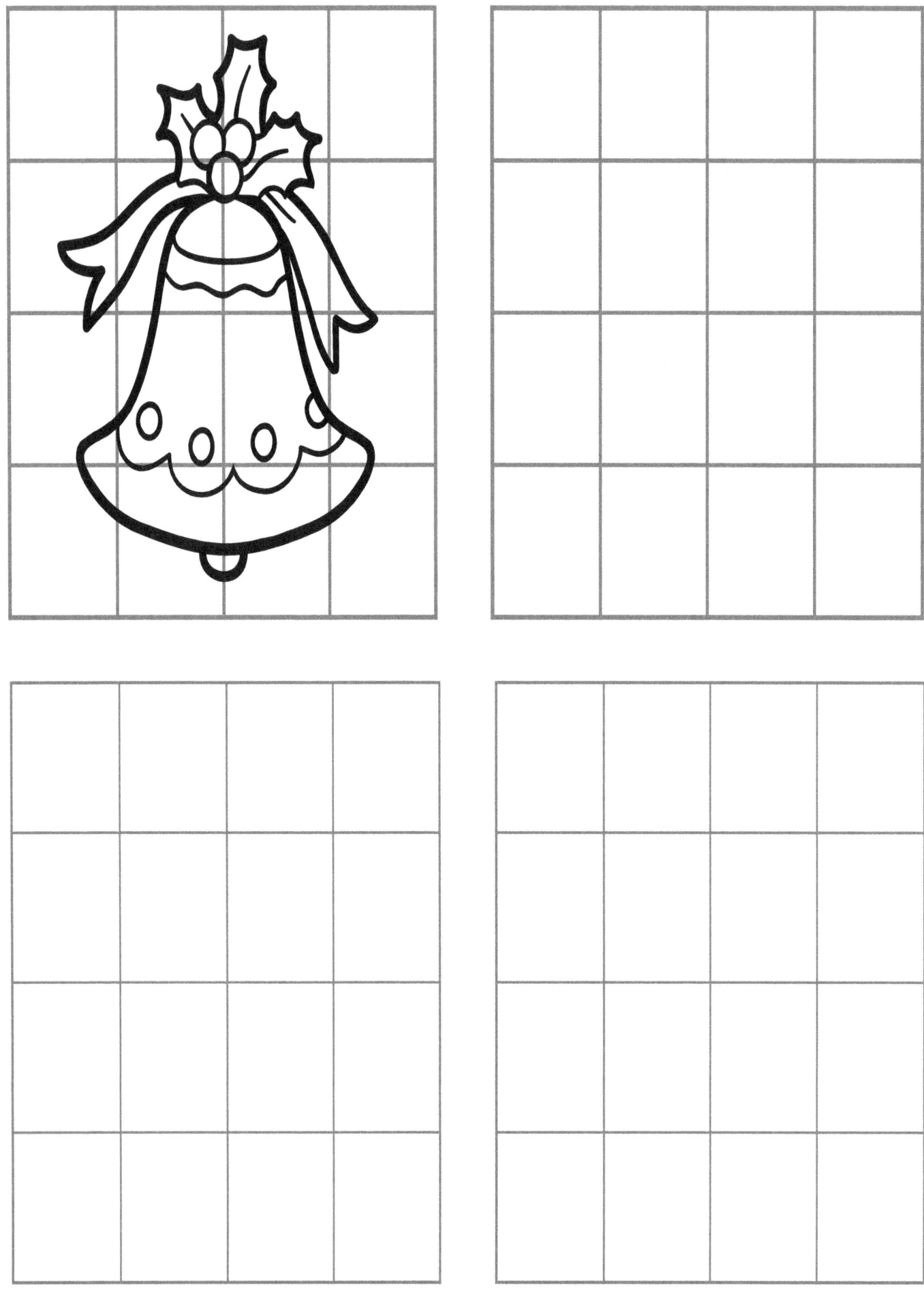

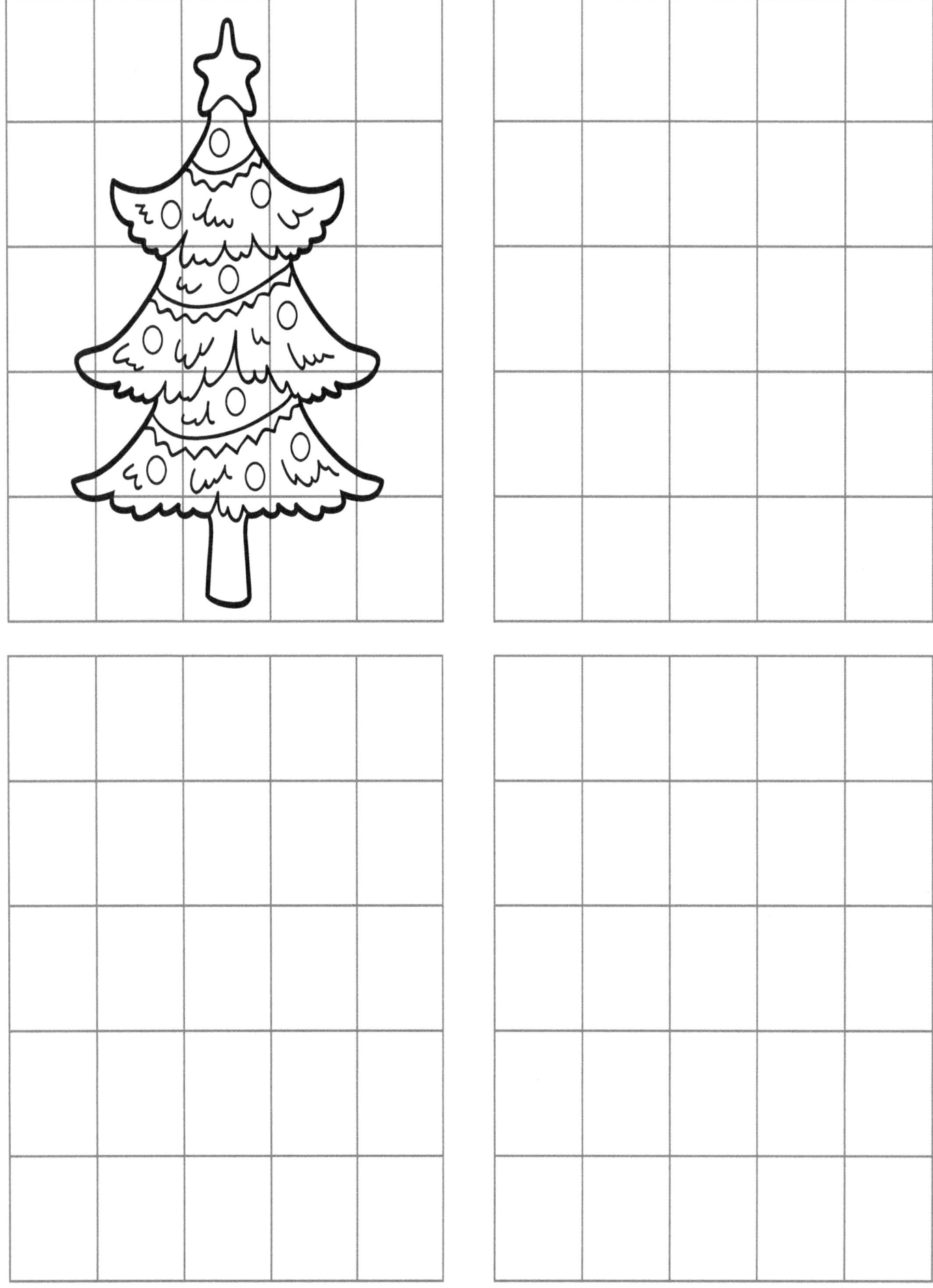

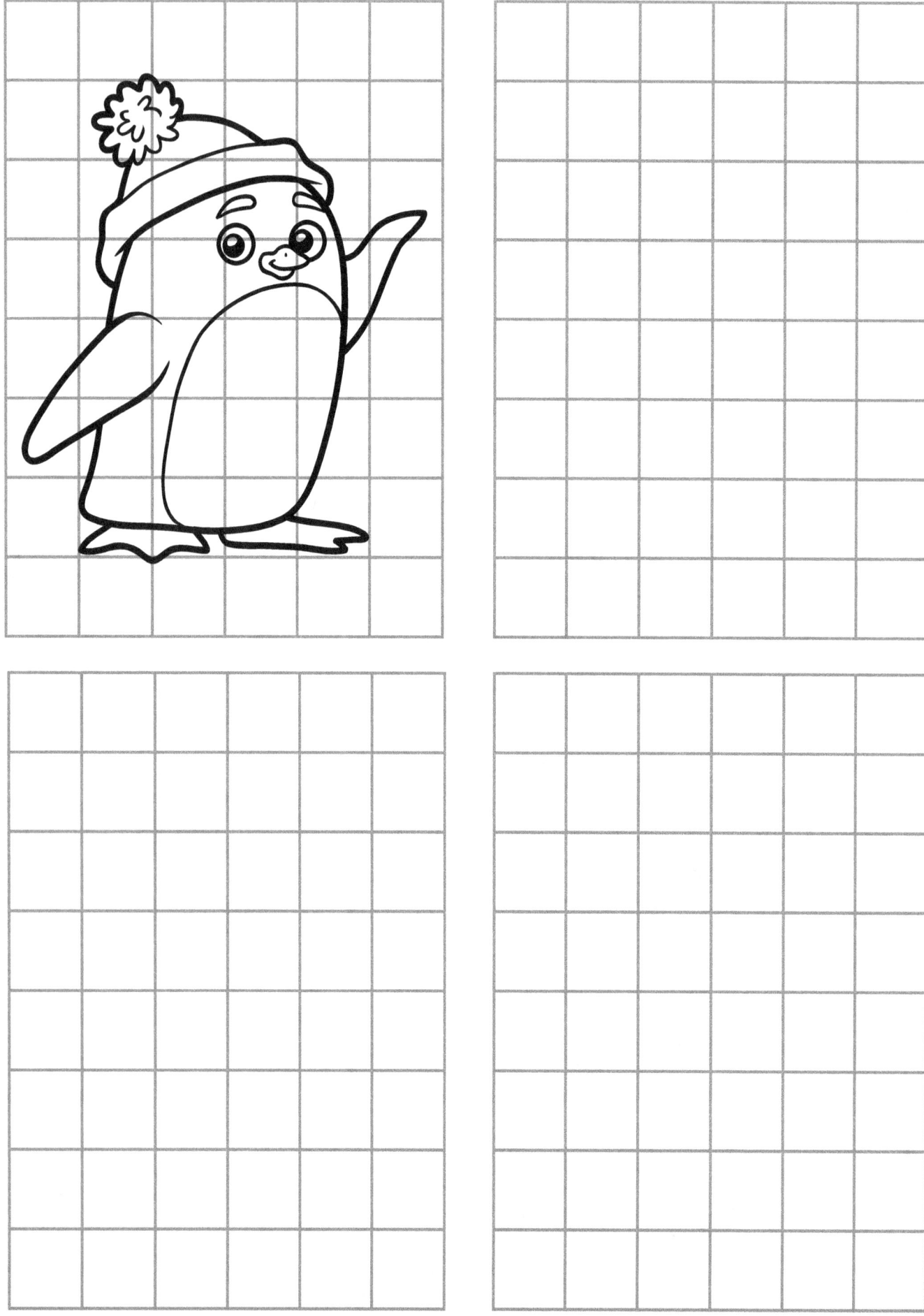

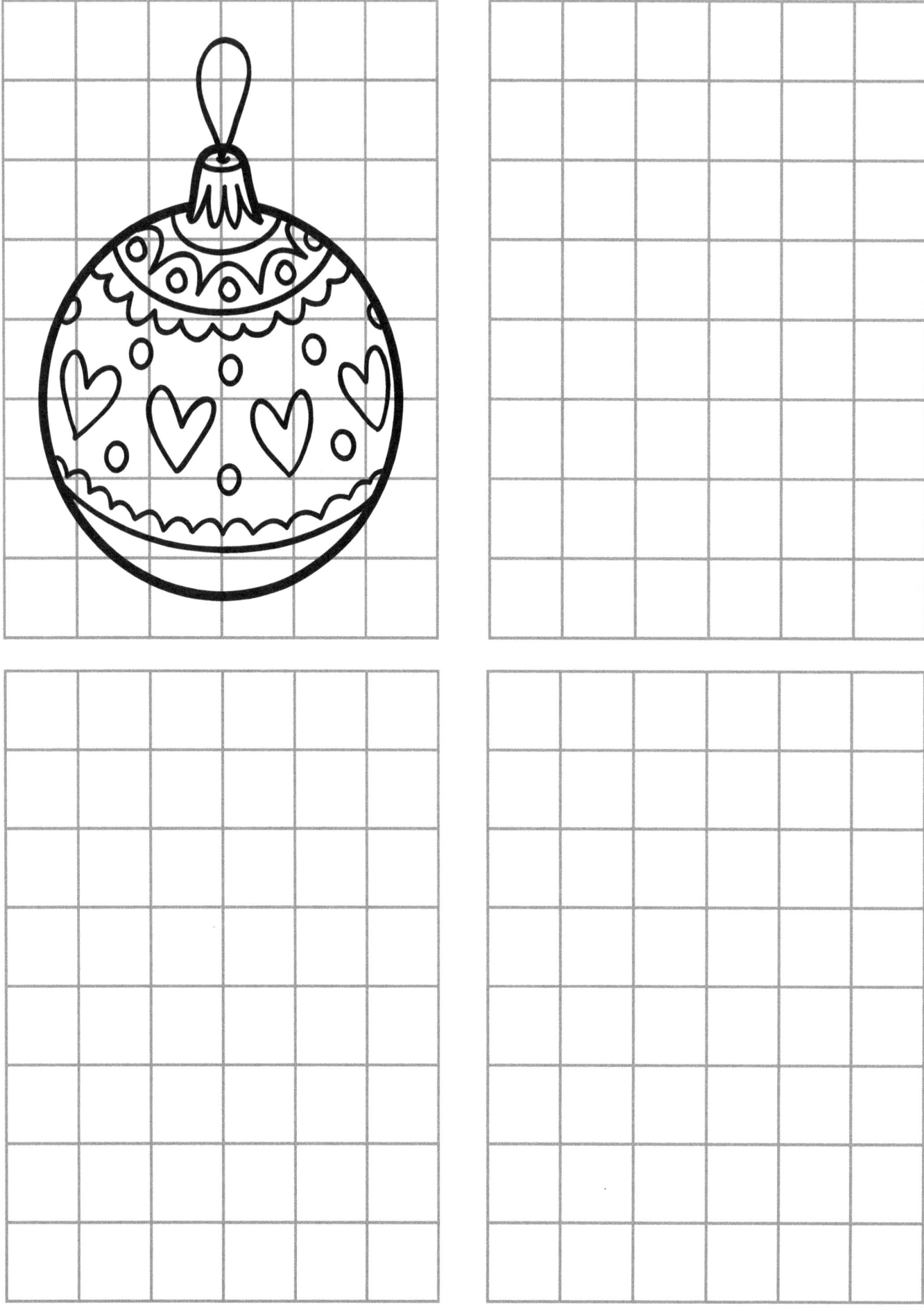

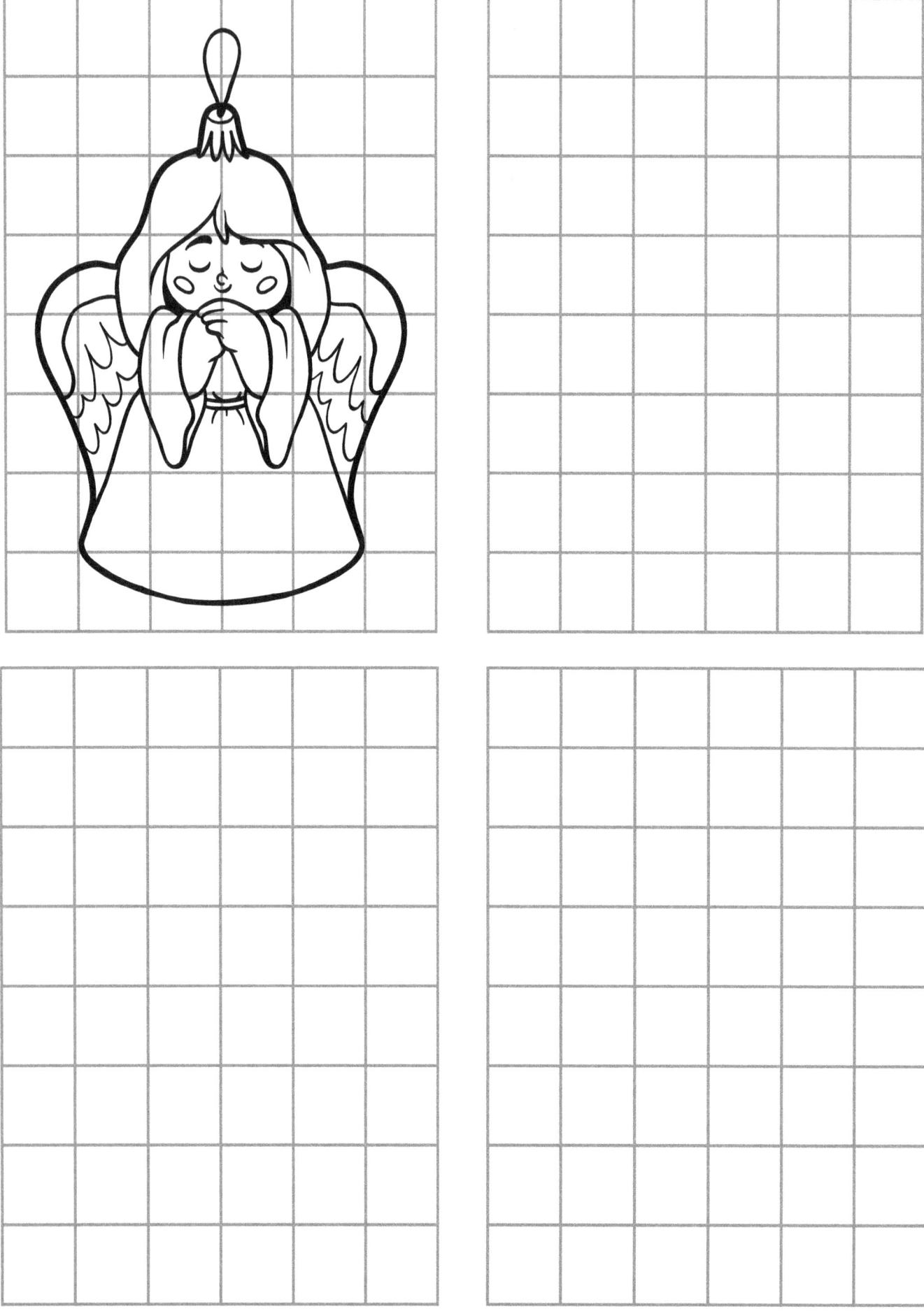

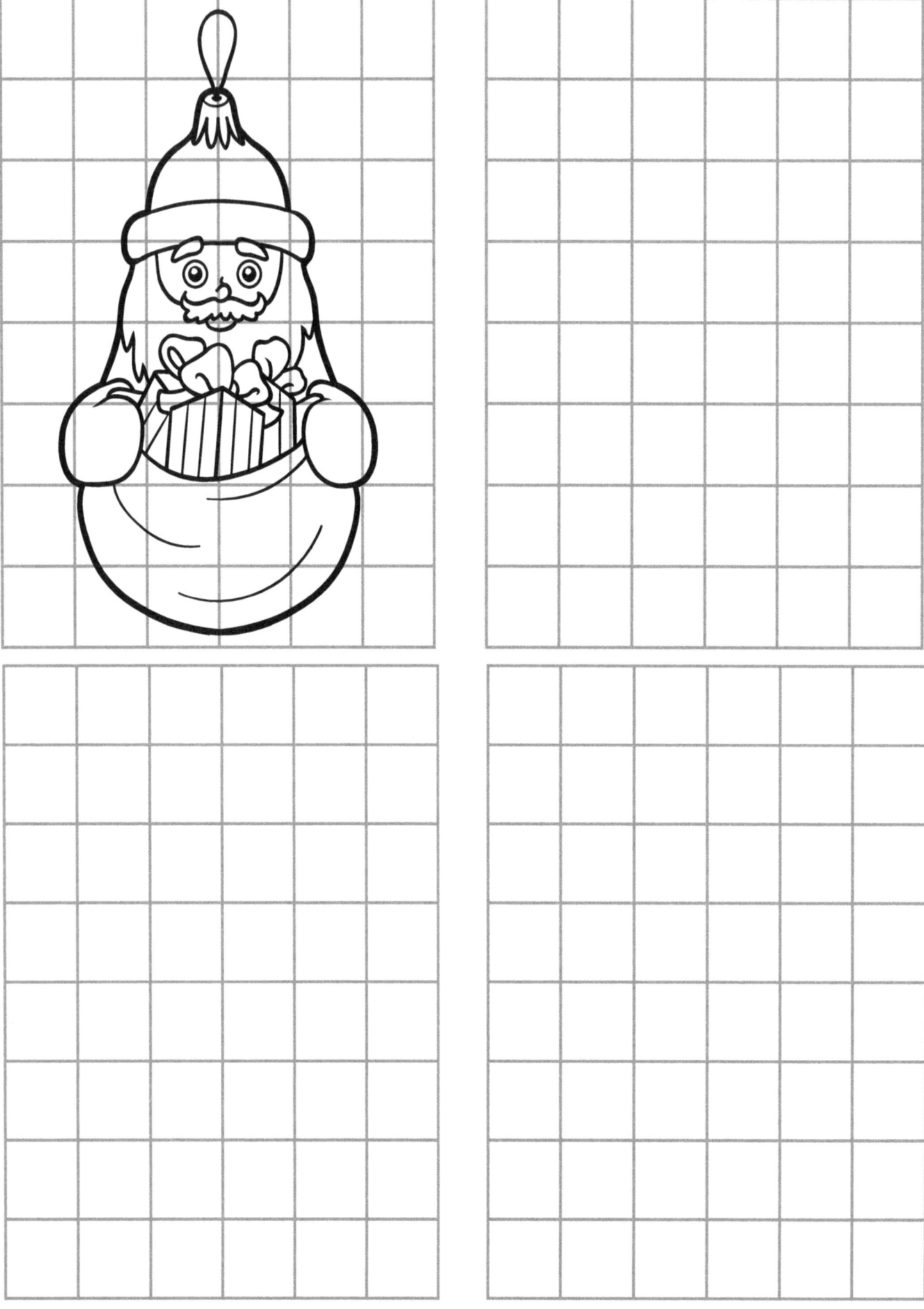

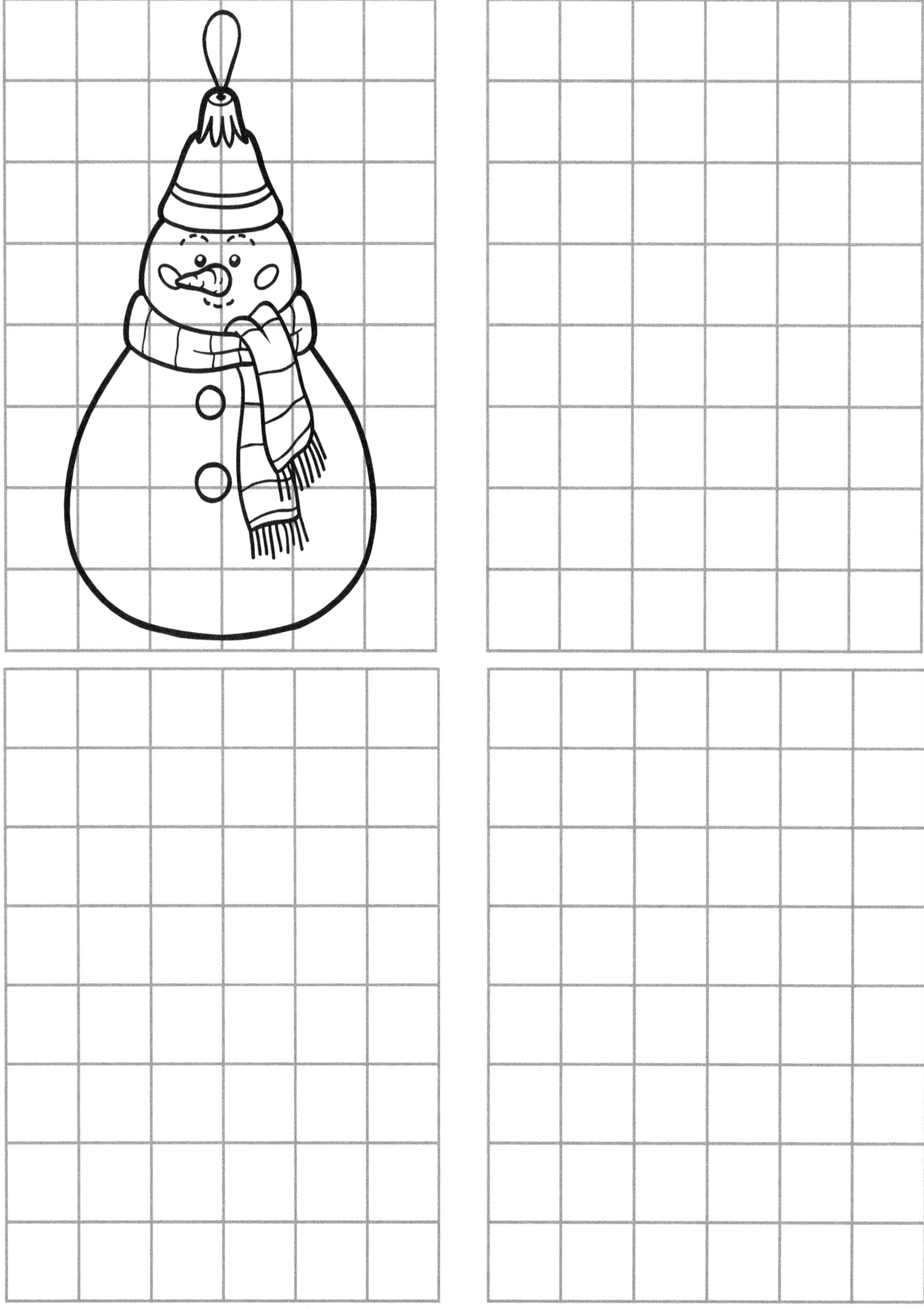

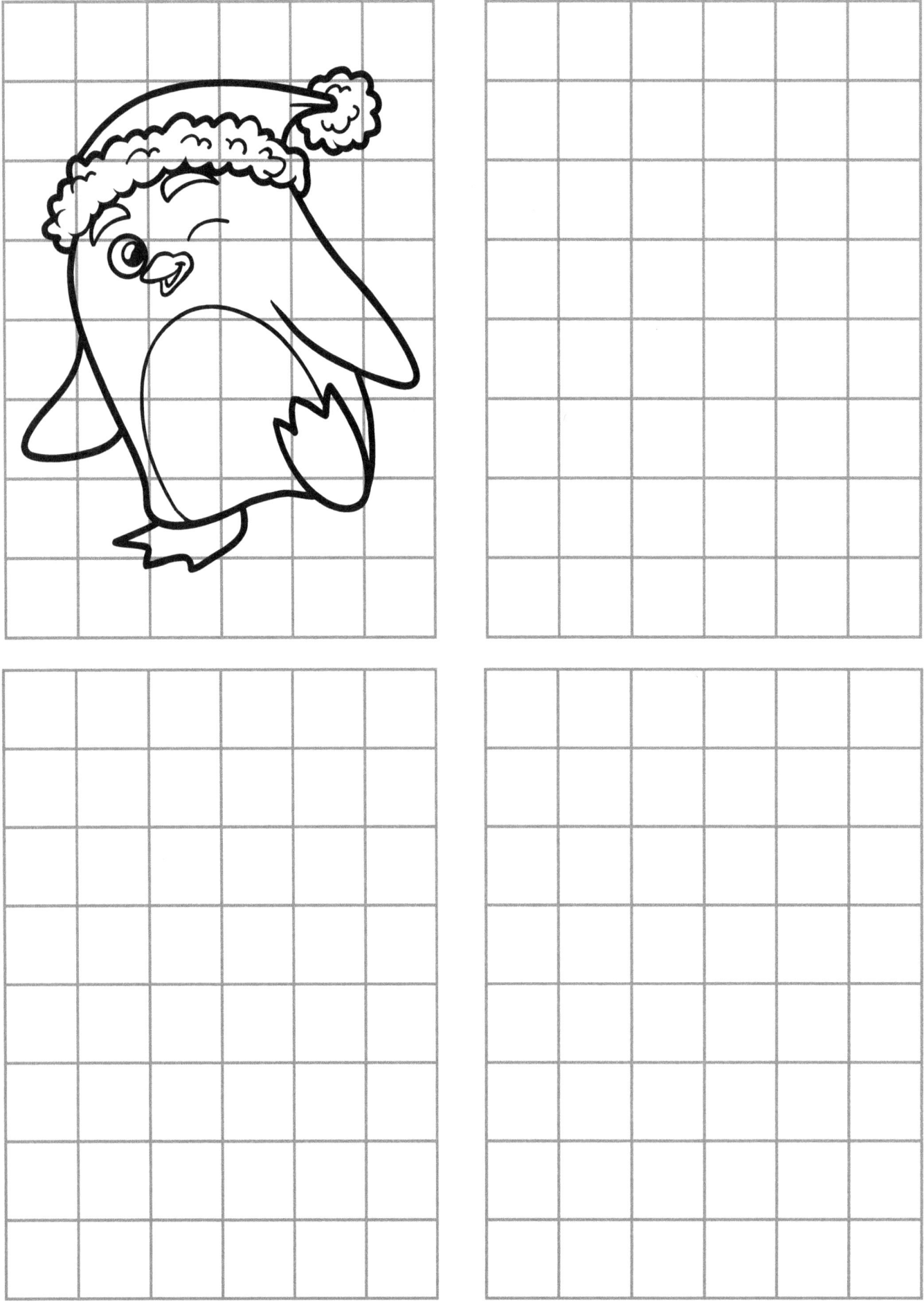

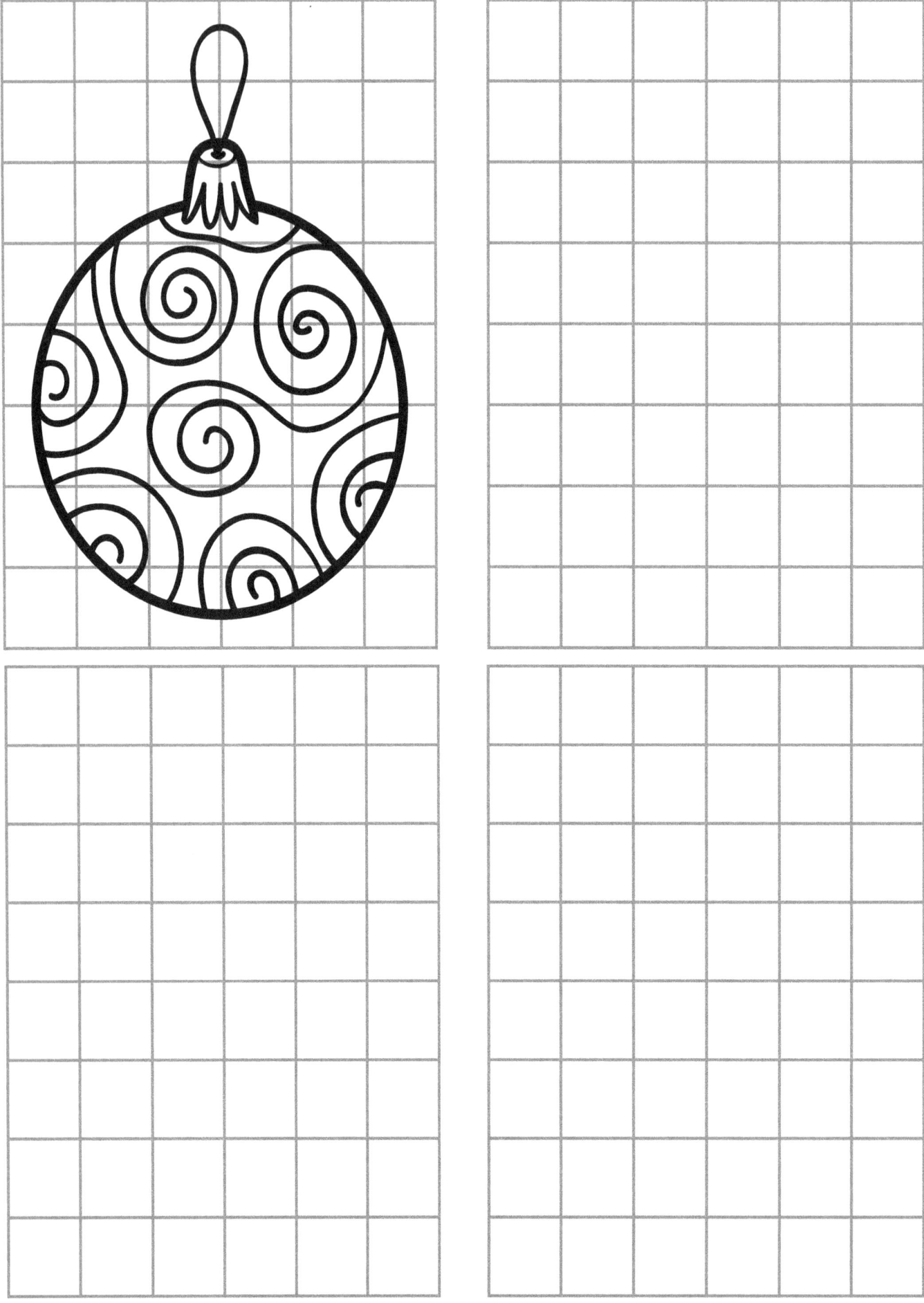

adventurelearningpress.com

www.ingramcontent.com/pod-product-compliance
Lightning Source LLC
Chambersburg PA
CBHW081759280526
45789CB00008B/2923